The Beast, His Image, and His Mark

Insights into Revelation, Book 2

Other Books by the Author

The Coming End of the Age

An Overview of the Endtime

Preparing For the Lord's Return

Greapa

The Coming of the King in Matthew 24 and 25

The Goal and Peak of Our Christian Experience
Insights into Revelation, Book 1

Firstfruits and Harvest
Insights into Revelation, Book 3

A Place Prepared
Insights into Revelation, Book 4

The Church in Philadelphia
Insights into Revelation, Book 5

Delusion and God's Salvation

A Faithful God

Booklets by the Author

The Heart of God	The Rapture
The Heart of God II	Urgency or Complacency
The Heart of God III	A New Creation
The Heart of God IV	The Spirit
The Heart of God V	The Spirit Was Not Yet
The Heart of God VI	The Lark Ascending
Redemption and Salvation	The Order of Melchizedek
Signs of the End	The Prayer of the End

Visit **aplaceinthewilderness.com** for more about these books (including their introduction, table of contents, and ordering information) and booklets.

The Beast, His Image, and His Mark

Insights into Revelation, Book 2

Paul Cozza

A Place in the Wilderness

THE BEAST, HIS IMAGE, AND HIS MARK
INSIGHTS INTO REVELATION, BOOK 2

© 2018 Paul Cozza

ISBN 978-1-5136-3776-1

All rights reserved. No part of this publication may be reproduced or transmitted in any form or by any means—electronic, mechanical, or any other, including photocopy, recording, or any information or retrieval system—without prior written consent, in hardcopy paper form, from:

Paul Cozza
A Place in the Wilderness

Website: aplaceinthewilderness.com
Email: paul@aplaceinthewilderness.com

Second printing: July, 2025

Scripture quotations are from the
American Standard Version of the Bible (1901)
unless otherwise noted.

Cover design: Nuggitz Creative Services (Nuggitz.com)
Globe network: © NicoElNino | iStockphoto.com
Man's face: © DmitryPoch | DepositPhotos.com

Table of Contents

Preface 1

Introduction 5
   Satan's Resistance 5
   The Hidden Plan 6
   The Role of Technology 7

Chapter 1 – A Synopsis 9
   The Great Leader 9
   Middle East Crisis 10
   The Covenant 11
   The First Half of the Final Seven Years 12
   Slain and Resuscitated 12
   The Last Half of the Final Seven Years 14
   Two Witnesses and Two Beasts 14
   Mysteries 16

Chapter 2 – Technology 21
   The Direction of Technology 21
   A Confluence 22
   Computing 22
   Quantum Computing 23
   Artificial Intelligence 24
   Virtual Reality 25
   MMOs 25
   Exoskeletons 25

Robotics 26

Communications 26

Neural Implants 26

The Overlord 27

Chapter 3 – The Abomination Revealed 29

The Beast and the AI Deity 29

The Image of the Beast 32

The Mark of the Beast 34

Delusion 34

The Abomination of Desolation 38

The Abomination of the Mark 39

The Abomination of the Beast 40

The Great Counterfeit 41

Chapter 4 – The Darkest Time 45

The Rapture 45

The Sixth Seal 46

The Two Witnesses 46

The 144,000 of Israel 46

The Antichrist Slain 47

The Flood of Judgment 47

The Abyss 49

Consolidating Power 50

The Second Beast 50

Jerusalem Surrounded 51

Locusts 51

War 53

Slaughter 54

Chapter 5 – God's Wisdom and Mercy 57
   Only One 57
   Delusion Revisited 57
   Great Tribulation 59
   The Consummation 60
   Israel's Fate 62

A Final Word 67

Note to the Reader:
Explanations and further details about the text appear as footnotes. Scripture references are cited in the numbered **References** list at the end of each chapter.

Preface

I wrote a first book about the endtime, a chronology of that period, in the mid-1990s. It describes all the major events that will occur at the end of this age. Fresh light from the Lord shone on many of the endtime happenings. The Lord opened that whole epoch before me in a new way, illuminating one important matter after another.

Now, more than twenty years later, I'm being drawn back to endtime events. The Lord is shining more light, and the world situation has changed considerably. Technology has advanced so rapidly that things once unthinkable are now possible and even predicted in the near future. I feel an urgency from the Lord to write what He is showing me in His Word and in the world.

My urgency is because this vision of endtime events must be shown to God's people. The time is so short, and our need is so great, yet the cloud of confusion regarding the Lord's return surrounds Christians today—a cloud sent from the evil one who would if possible keep every Christian in darkness.

But the dark age is ending! The Lord is speaking today; His light is shining. Today we're in the book of Revelation where the Spirit is not simply the one Spirit;[1] today He is the seven Spirits,[2] the Spirit that has been intensified and amplified to meet every need in the current extreme darkness enveloping the earth. The shining of the seven Spirits is the remedy for the darkness and confusion many believers suffer today. And so I write to release what has been given to me.

In this current book series, I'm explicating certain crucial events in the book of Revelation. In the first book[*] of the series, the great happenings in Revelation 12 and 14 are opened in a new way. This is the Lord's call to His people. He is drawing His seekers to the one "place" that is the goal and the peak of the Christian experience. He desires every Christian to attain to that, and so

---

[*] *The Goal and Peak of Our Christian Experience.*

He's opening the heavens to show and attract us to our ultimate goal.

As He opens our eyes to who He is and what He's doing, we are drawn, moved to seek Him and run after Him. He is too beautiful! What He presents to us in Revelation 14 is unbearably attractive; to gain that which is before us is worth far more than all that we are, all that we have, our future, our past, and everything about us!

Yet as high and as positive as the first book is, there's a low, a negative, that's the worst that will ever happen to mankind. The Lord is speaking details about this as well, as an urgent warning to all the earth concerning what's about to occur.

It's true that God's judgments—as seen in the sixth and seventh seals and the seven trumpets in Revelation—are about to strike the earth. This may well happen within the next fifteen or twenty years; based upon the world situation, it's a near certainty that it will occur within the next fifty. But I am not writing of these judgments here.[*]

This book deals with the evil that's rapidly growing on the earth and will be fully manifested before the Lord returns. We're told that eventually the man of sin, the lawless one, will be revealed.[3] He'll sit in the temple claiming to be God. He's called the "beast"[4] in the book of Revelation, for so he is. In addition, there are certain aspects of his coming—specifically his mark and his image—that must be more fully explained. For that purpose, this book is written. It deals especially with Revelation 13, although it also touches other important sections of Revelation and the prophecies of Daniel, in order to provide a clear vision of what the endtime will be like for those dwelling on the earth, for Europe more particularly, and for Israel specifically.

I freely admit that a good portion of what's in this book cannot be found directly in God's Word. Some may say that this is merely speculation or opinion on my part. But consider this: at the time the Bible was written, it was simply not possible to convey in God's Word today's technology and the technology that will be

---

[*] These were more fully detailed in a second short book I recently wrote, *Preparing for the Lord's Return.*

available at the close of this age. Virtually every single item of today's technology had not even entered into the mind of any man upon the face of the earth. Not only were today's inventions non-existent, but man had not yet even imagined the concepts behind them. As a consequence, there simply were no words in existence to write of what science is producing today. To those in biblical times, practically everything in our current technology would have seemed miraculous, magical, or demonic. Could they have understood an automobile? They would have thought it magical. A computer? They would have considered that wizardry. By necessity, all modern technology has been left out of the Bible, but that doesn't mean it's neither implied nor present there.

But the Lord would not leave us in the dark concerning technology. The Lord is still speaking today, still shining in His Word and on the world situation, and still warning His people. Therefore, I ask the reader of this book to bear with my digression into technological areas that aren't found in God's Word. Bear with me and pray. Pray over these matters to see whether the Lord would speak to you in them. In this book, you may find both crucial insights into the final years of this age and a timely warning for the future.

I believe that what I'm writing is accurate enough to convey the deeply troubling vision of the endtime events concerning the beast, his image, and his mark, in order to inform and warn us. May the Lord speak to you in these words, even as He has spoken to me in the vision before my eyes.

References

[1] Eph. 4:4
[2] Rev. 1:4
[3] 2 Thes. 2:3
[4] Rev. 11:7; 13:1-4, 11-18

Introduction

Throughout the seemingly countless eons since Satan's first rebellion, God has been working slowly and inexorably to limit Satan and eventually cast him into the lake of fire for eternity. However, limiting a spirit such as Satan is not simple. How do you limit that which has no physicality? How do you even locate a spirit?

God is not without His means, however. While a spirit does not have physicality, it can be bound by its own nature and by its psychological and spiritual attachments. Using such means, God over time limited Satan and his followers to the earth, and in particular to the sky above the earth.[1] While Satan continues to have access to God at His throne,[2] he's now bound to the earth.

God further limited Satan when man fell. In order to bring about man's fall, Satan injected something of himself into man—what the apostle Paul calls sin.[3] According to Paul, sin is the satanic nature within man. Paul describes it as dwelling in us,[4] working in us,[5] and beguiling and killing us,[6] among other things. All these are the actions of a person, and they describe the operation of that satanic nature in us.

However, by injecting his nature into man, Satan also bound himself to man. God used this to bring Satan to nought,[7] for when Christ died upon the cross, He brought to the cross with Him all mankind[8] with the indwelling satanic nature. As a result, today in the Spirit the cross is the death knell for Satan.

Satan's Resistance

Satan, of course, uses all his power and every means at his disposal to resist God's move. After all, that's his nature—he's a rebel and the father of rebellion. Since the creation of man, he has worked incessantly to thwart God's plan with man. He knows that it is man whom God will use to both overcome him and put an end to his rule.

Satan's desire is to destroy man, for it is man who challenges his reign. Destroying man would allow Satan to continue indefinitely. But God would not allow Satan to destroy man directly. Indeed, Satan requires God's permission to touch a man directly.[9] However, Satan has other means for bringing about man's demise.

Satan either works to so corrupt man that God intervenes and destroys man, or he works within man in an attempt to induce man to destroy himself. The days of Noah[10] are an example of the former. The satanic forces instigated so much violence upon the earth by mingling themselves with the daughters of men[11] that God intervened, destroying the whole inhabited earth.[12] But Noah found grace in the eyes of the Lord,[13] and through Noah and his family the human race was saved. Satan's plan was thus thwarted.

We have examples of Satan inducing man to destroy himself as well. The development of immensely destructive nuclear weapons no doubt had the evil one as its source, as he plotted to cause man's annihilation. The 1963 Cuban missile crisis brought the whole world to the brink of catastrophic nuclear war. Only the Lord knows what the outcome of a full-scale nuclear war would have been at that time, but the Lord intervened and did not allow it.

We have another such example during the endtime. The violence and destruction then will be so great that no flesh would survive except the Lord shorten those days.[14] He will intervene once again to save mankind, and Israel in particular.

The Hidden Plan

Hidden within Satan's primary plot to destroy man is his plan B, his subtle attempt to exalt himself above God through man. If he can subjugate man—bring man to the point where man worships him rather than God—then he can declare victory. He can force God to either destroy man entirely or to subject Himself to Satan on earth. For man's choice is the deciding factor on earth, since God gave man dominion over all the earth,[15] and God would not renege on such a promise.

God is righteous. Everything He does is proper, right in every sense. He doesn't lie, cheat, or attempt to force others to His will. Satan is the antithesis of God; he lies, cheats, steals, murders, rapes, and attempts to force everyone to obey his will. There's nothing in him or about him that is proper. No single deed of his is righteous. Therefore it shouldn't be surprising that Satan will use every means possible to persuade, induce, or compel man to worship him. He knows to not go beyond the bounds God has set for his actions, for in doing so he would suffer immediate judgment from God. But within those bounds, Satan is without restraint—completely lawless.

Perhaps more disconcerting is the fact that as the endtime approaches, the One who has restrained lawlessness on the earth for millennia* will no longer do so.[16] This means that lawlessness will increase, abound, and eventually run amok. Even today we see this in the atheism and godless extremism that are rampant upon the earth. We see it in the hatred toward God, toward Christ, toward Christians, and toward anything related to God. This is Satan unleashed upon the earth. And this lawlessness will become much worse as the day of the Lord's return approaches.

As that day nears, Satan will release his masterpiece, his final attempt to subjugate and ultimately destroy man. This will be his plot within a plot, his plan B. When that time comes, the environment will be unspeakably brutal, especially to those living in Israel. Were it not for the Lord, not one human being would survive.

The Role of Technology

This book centers on Revelation 13, where the monstrous elements of Satan's plan are revealed. While most of what's there could be dismissed as satanic wonders or merely natural happenings, seeing what is occurring on the earth today leads me to believe that this is not the case. I believe technology will play a prominent role in Satan's endtime plot. Furthermore, as the day approaches, the role of technology will become even clearer.

I've endeavored in this book to present what I see. I leave it to the reader and the reader's prayers to determine before the Lord the accuracy of what I present here. I'm not a prophet in the sense

---

* This should refer to the Holy Spirit in His restraining power in the world.

of one foretelling the future, but I firmly believe that what I present in this book will be substantially the same as what occurs during the last few years of this age. May this book be an enlightenment and a warning to all God's people.

References

[1] Eph. 2:2
[2] Rev. 12:10
[3] Rom. 5:12
[4] Rom. 7:17, 20
[5] Rom. 7:13
[6] Rom. 7.11
[7] Heb. 2:14
[8] Gal. 2:20; 6:14
[9] Job 1:12; 2:4-6
[10] Gen. 6:12-13
[11] Gen. 6:1-2
[12] Gen. 6:7
[13] Gen. 6:8
[14] Matt. 24:22
[15] Gen. 1:28
[16] 2 Thes. 2:6-7

CHAPTER 1

A Synopsis

And I saw a beast coming up out of the sea, having ten horns and seven heads, and on his horns ten diadems, and upon his heads names of blasphemy. (Rev. 13:1)

Revelation 13 speaks of a person called the "beast." Prophecy in both the Old and New Testaments says more about this person than any other in history (except the Lord Jesus Himself). The Word of God doesn't leave us in darkness concerning this man who'll arise near the end of this age.

He's called by many names, all referring to the same person. In Daniel 7–8, he's called "the little horn."[1] In Daniel 9, he is "the prince that shall come."[2] In Daniel 11–12, he is "the king of the north."[3] In Revelation 9, he is "Abaddon and Apollyon."[4] He's also referred to as "the man of sin" in 2 Thessalonians.[5] Interestingly, the name by which he is most commonly known—the Antichrist—is not used in the Bible to refer to him directly.

The Great Leader

Thus he said, The fourth beast shall be a fourth kingdom upon earth, which shall be diverse from all the kingdoms, and shall devour the whole earth, and shall tread it down, and break it in pieces. And as for the ten horns, out of this kingdom shall ten kings arise; and another shall arise after them; and he shall be diverse from the former, and he shall put down three kings. (Dan. 7:23-24)

And I saw a beast coming up out of the sea, having ten horns and seven heads, and on his horns ten diadems, and upon his heads names of blasphemy. (Rev. 13:1)

And the ten horns that thou sawest are ten kings, who have received no kingdom as yet; but they receive authority as kings, with the beast, for one hour. (Rev. 17:12)

Throughout all human history, there has never been a person like this one[6] who is coming. He'll seem to rise out of nowhere,[7] without notoriety or notable credentials. When he appears, he'll quickly seize control of the whole ten-nation alliance[8] along the Mediterranean that will exist in Europe at that time. He'll rapidly morph from a virtual unknown to the supreme leader of the ten-nation empire. He'll be extraordinary in every way. There will be no one to match him.

However, his rise to power within his empire will not be without resistance. The leaders of at least three[9] of these ten nations will oppose him, but he'll overcome and subdue them. Eventually, after having put down all resistance, he'll reign over an empire in southern Europe centered around Rome; it will be a revived Roman Empire, a modern reincarnation of the empire that existed about two thousand years ago. This is clearly described in the prophecies of both Daniel and Revelation.

He'll be astute, brilliant, and able to solve puzzles and understand dark sayings.[10] He'll have an unmatched mind, particularly for a politician. Nobody will be able to stand against his perception, insight, and intuition.

In addition, he'll be a phenomenal military leader, an unrivaled military strategist.[11] He'll expand toward the east, toward the south, and toward Israel.[12] No one will be able to stand against him militarily. It will be as if he can see into the future, knowing exactly what his enemies will do. On the battlefield, he'll be unbeatable. Indeed, people on the earth will say, "Who is able to war with him?"[13]

Middle East Crisis

We don't know how long it will be from the time the beast arises in his empire until the end of the age, but it appears to be a very short time. At some point after he seizes power, there will apparently be an extreme crisis* in the Middle East. It might be that all-out war between Arab nations and Israel seems inevitable. Israel might threaten the use of nuclear weapons if attacked. The whole world might once again be brought to the brink of nuclear war, as nations side either with the Arabs or Israel. The severity of that crisis and the intense worldwide pressure accompanying it cannot be overstated.

The Covenant

And he shall make a firm covenant with many for one week. (Dan. 9:27)

It's at this point that the one called "the beast" will exhibit his extraordinary abilities to seemingly solve the entire Mideast problem.† He'll devise a solution to the Mideast situation that seems to end all the conflicts existing there today. With respect to Israel, his solution might require the denuclearization of Israel's military. Such a concession on Israel's part would satisfy the Arab nations surrounding her. What Israel will get in return for such a concession might be, among other things, a security guarantee by this great European leader and the freedom to reconstruct the temple on the freshly "available" Temple Mount.

This "coming prince" will negotiate a covenant with Israel, which may include the Arab nations as well. It should be ratified by a referendum in Israel through which the majority of Israelis— the "many"[14]—agree to the covenant. The pact will last for 2,520 days, or seven biblical years of 360 days each. The events leading up to these seven years at the end of this age are shown in sequence in the following graphic.

---

* Based upon the current world situation and what must occur according to prophecy during the endtime, this crisis might be caused by the destruction of the Al-Aqsa Mosque on the Temple Mount in Jerusalem.

† Indeed, he was probably waiting for just this moment to demonstrate these skills.

Events Preceding the Endtime

Ten-nation alliance comes into being (Dan. 7:7)

↓

The "little horn" arises and seizes power (Dan. 7:8)

↓

Crisis in the Middle East

↓

Covenant between the coming prince and Israel for the last of Daniel's seventy weeks (Dan. 9:27)

The First Half of the Final Seven Years

A number of important things crucial to the endtime should occur during the first half of that last seven biblical years: Israel will rid herself of nuclear weapons; forces from the ten-nation European empire will be stationed in Israel, and particularly Jerusalem, to guarantee Israel's security; the Temple Mount will be cleared of debris remaining from destruction of the Al-Aqsa Mosque; the Old Testament animal sacrifices will be reinstituted; the temple will be rebuilt.

Slain and Resuscitated

And I saw one of his heads as though it had been smitten unto death; and his death-stroke was healed... (Rev. 13:3)

Near the middle of the seven-year pact, the temple will be completed. However, something extraordinary and seemingly miraculous will occur. The beast will be slain by the sword.[15] He'll be killed and yet not remain dead.[16] Behind the scenes in the spiritual realm, invisible to human eyes, Satan will release the spirit of the one called Abbadon and Apollyon[17] (who is actually the spirit of Caesar Nero). This spirit will inhabit the body of the dead beast, resuscitating him and bringing him back to life. He'll apparently be resurrected.

While this may sound far-fetched, it is scriptural and quite logical. It is said of the beast that in John's time he already *was*[18] (past tense). Therefore, the coming beast must be someone who existed before John wrote Revelation. It goes on to say that he *was not*, as John was writing Revelation. So when he wrote this book, the one who previously *was* must have died, because he no longer was. Yet he was coming and about to rise from out of the abyss.[19] That is, the one who was and died would come again, and he would again come up out of the abyss where the spirits of some of the dead are kept. So the beast is someone who lived before John wrote Revelation, but was not alive not at the time he wrote it—and he would live again at some future point. This means that the beast is someone who had died by the time of the writing of Revelation.

John also says that the readers of Revelation could understand who the beast is and what his number means.[20] This indicates that the beast is a prominent person known to the believers in the apostle John's day. Furthermore, the number of this beast is specified: 666. If we add the numbers associated with the letters of Caesar Nero's name in Hebrew, they add up to 666:

English		Greek		Hebrew		Number
Ne	→	Νε	→	נ	→	50
r	→	ρ	→	ר	→	200
o	→	ο	→	ו	→	6
n	→	ν	→	נ	→	50
Kai	→	Και	→	ק	→	100
sa	→	σα	→	ס	→	60
r	→	ρ	→	ר	→	200
				Total	=	666

In addition to being an extraordinary leader, after his death and resuscitation he'll be something quite unnatural, peculiar, even monstrous. He'll be the body of the great European leader who was killed, resuscitated by the spirit of Caesar Nero, who'll be brought up out of the abyss by Satan[21] at the middle of the seven-year pact between Israel and this leader.

The Last Half of the Final Seven Years

In brief, up to the middle of the seven-year pact, the European leader is extraordinary but merely human. After he's slain and rises again, he's something much more—a human being now inhabited by the spirit of Caesar Nero, perhaps the most vile, despicable, murderous, abominable person who ever walked the face of the earth.

Those final three and a half years on the earth (for which more detail will be provided in chapters 3 and 4) will be a time like no other. It will be a period of extreme angst, anguish, and torment—spiritually, psychologically, physically. The spiritual battle between the satanic forces and God will rage incessantly. This war will be for the hearts, minds, and spirits of men—for Israel specifically and for mankind generally.

At the beginning of the last three and a half years of the age, the resuscitated beast will break the covenant with Israel. He'll end the animal sacrifices and commence tormenting the Jews. This monstrous being will do what he always did—destroy. In Rome, Nero was the first to burn the Christians. He initiated the war against the rebelling Jews, which essentially ended with the destruction of Jerusalem. He's thought by many to have burned his own capital, Rome. He committed suicide in 68 A.D. At the end of the age, in the body of the great European leader, he will do according to his nature—torment and kill God's people, and destroy.

Two Witnesses and Two Beasts

And I will give unto my two witnesses, and they shall prophesy a thousand two hundred and threescore days, clothed in sackcloth. These are the two olive trees and the two candlesticks, standing before the Lord of the earth. And if any man desireth to hurt them, fire proceedeth out of their mouth and devoureth their enemies; and if any man shall desire to hurt them, in this manner must he be killed. These have the power to shut the heaven, that it rain not during the days of their prophecy: and they have power over the waters to turn them into blood, and to smite the earth with every plague, as often as they shall desire. (Rev. 11:3-6)

And I saw a beast coming up out of the sea, having ten horns and seven heads, and on his horns ten diadems, and upon his heads names of blasphemy. (Rev 13:1)

And I saw another beast coming up out of the earth; and he had two horns like unto a lamb, and he spake as a dragon. (Rev. 13:11)

At the beginning of this final three and a half years, God will send Moses and Elijah* back to Israel as a testimony to the Jews. In response to this introduction by God of the two witnesses into the situation in Israel, Satan will make a countermove. It's always Satan's way to mimic God by using that which is false but which resembles God's way in appearance.

I believe that before these things take place, there'll have been a discussion between Satan and God in the heavens. Satan may dispute God's right to send the two witnesses back to Israel. Moses had died, and Elisha had been taken from the earth by God. Satan may ask God what gives Him the right to send either man back to Israel a second time. To send them back would be something supernatural, against natural law. Perhaps Satan will demand the permission from God to do something similar, or perhaps God will offer. Whatever the case, Satan will be granted the authority to bring back two of his choosing, just as God will bring back Moses and Elijah.

As we've seen, Caesar Nero will be one of the two the devil will select. Nero may be the most evil leader that has ever lived, an appropriate choice for Satan. The second will be the one called the false prophet,[22] the beast's cohort. A number of Bible scholars

---

* In the Old Testament, God promised to send Elijah back to Israel before His coming (Mal. 4:5). This was confirmed by the Lord when He was on the earth (Matt. 17:11). While there has been some dispute about the identity of the second of the two witnesses, it's apparent from the behavior (Rev. 11:6) of these two witnesses that the second must be Moses. Michael disputed with Satan about Moses' body (Jude 1:9) because it would be needed for just this coming moment. Additionally, it was Moses and Elijah who appeared with the Lord on the Mount of Transfiguration to speak with Him about His death (Luke 9:30-31).

have thought this person to be Judas Iscariot* returned from the dead, and this would be quite fitting—the most evil person and the greatest betrayer in league to destroy God's people.

In addition to the physical, psychological, and spiritual warfare raging at this time, there'll be yet another aspect to the intense battle being fought between God and Satan. That will be the battle for the hearts of the Jews, a battle in which Moses and Elijah will oppose the beast and the false prophet.

Satan will also use some other extraordinary methods to entice, cajole, and coerce men to follow and worship him. The first of these will be an idol set up in the newly constructed temple by the false prophet. This will be no typical idol made of stone, wood, or gold. This idol will be given breath by the false prophet—it will talk. Furthermore, it will kill men and compel them to worship it.

There's one other thing of great import that Satan will use: the mark of the beast. For centuries, those who study Revelation have assumed that this will be a simple mark on the hand or forehead, either the name or number of the beast. However, I believe there's something much deeper here.

Mysteries

Neither shall he regard the gods of his fathers, nor the desire of women, nor regard any god; for he shall magnify himself above all. But in his place shall he honor the god of fortresses; and a god whom his fathers knew not shall he honor with gold, and silver, and with precious stones and pleasant things. And he shall deal with the strongest fortresses by the help of a foreign god. (Dan. 11:37-39)

And he deceiveth them that dwell on the earth by reason of the signs which it was given him to do in the sight of the beast; saying

---

* When Judas Iscariot died, has was not gathered to his people as other Old Testament people were (Gen. 25:8, 17; 35:29; 49:29; etc.). Rather, he went to his own place (Acts 1:25). This implied that Judas's death was something different; he was to be kept for a future point for some reason. In addition, what was it that Satan offered Judas to betray the Lord Jesus? It must have been something extraordinary for him to betray the Son of God. The rule over Israel during the endtime would have been just such an enticement for the fully corrupted Judas.

to them that dwell on the earth, that they should make an image to the beast who hath the stroke of the sword and lived. And it was given unto him to give breath to it, even to the image of the beast, that the image of the beast should both speak, and cause that as many as should not worship the image of the beast should be killed. (Rev. 13:14-15)

And he causeth all, the small and the great, and the rich and the poor, and the free and the bond, that there be given them a mark on their right hand, or upon their forehead; and that no man should be able to buy or to sell, save he that hath the mark, even the name of the beast or the number of his name. (Rev. 13:16-17)

And another angel, a third, followed them, saying with a great voice, If any man worshippeth the beast and his image, and receiveth a mark on his forehead, or upon his hand, he also shall drink of the wine of the wrath of God, which is prepared unmixed in the cup of his anger; and he shall be tormented with fire and brimstone in the presence of the holy angels, and in the presence of the Lamb: and the smoke of their torment goeth up for ever and ever; and they have no rest day and night, they that worship the beast and his image, and whoso receiveth the mark of his name. (Rev. 14:9-11)

While much has been revealed regarding the beast, his mark, and the idol in the temple, there are yet puzzles and mysteries concerning these. In Daniel 11, the beast is said to regard neither the gods of his fathers nor any god. And yet in the same verses we're told that he'll honor the god of fortresses, a god his fathers knew not. He'll also overcome fortresses with the help of a foreign god. These verses seem contradictory. They say that he will regard no god, yet he honors a god and is helped by a god. Furthermore, how can a foreign god be used to overcome strongholds?

Until this very year, these verses have been shrouded in mystery. I believe, however, that the solution to this puzzle is being revealed before our eyes as we watch what's occurring on the earth today.

Consider the mark of the beast. What kind of mark could prohibit men from buying and selling? It would seem, as has always been the case, that the black market would be able to circumvent any kind of restrictions based solely upon a mark on someone's skin. In addition, it's said that those who receive this mark will be tormented with fire eternally. What mark on the skin could warrant such eternal punishment? While it's true that this mark indicates an acceptance of the beast as a god and lord, it's also true that every sin and blasphemy will be forgiven to men.[23] What is it about this mark that apparently precludes the possibility of repentance once it's received, with no escape from eternal fire?

Finally, as we've seen, the image of the beast in the temple is mysterious. It will talk, compel, and kill. No created image has ever been able to do such things. Furthermore, both Daniel the prophet[24] and the Lord Jesus Himself[25]* speak of this image as the abomination of desolation. What is it that generates this image's utter and unprecedented distinctiveness, so that it's called an abomination?

Today the Lord is speaking, enlightening, and warning. He is revealing what's about to happen on the earth. I doubt that any of us fully realize just how severe, how dismal, how evil, how dark, how terrible and terrifying those last years will be. They'll come as a snare upon the whole earth, catching mankind in a trap from which there is seemingly no escape.

References

[1] Dan. 7:8; 8:9
[2] Dan. 9:27
[3] Dan. 11:40
[4] Rev. 9:11
[5] 2 Thes. 2:3
[6] Rev. 13:4
[7] Dan. 7:8, 24
[8] Rev. 17:12-13
[9] Dan. 7:8, 24
[10] Dan. 7:8, 8:23

---

* The Lord's word in Matthew 24:15 confirmed both Daniel's existence and his standing as a prophet. Those who dispute the veracity of the book of Daniel are thus exposed as unbelievers and disseminators of lies.

[11] Dan. 8:9-12, 23-25
[12] Dan. 8:9
[13] Rev. 13:4
[14] Dan. 9:27
[15] Rev. 13:14
[16] Rev. 13:3, 12, 14
[17] Rev. 9:1-2, 11
[18] Rev. 17:8
[19] Rev. 11:7; 17:8
[20] Rev. 13:18
[21] Rev. 9:11
[22] Rev. 16:13
[23] Matt 12:31
[24] Dan. 11:31; 12:11
[25] Matt. 24:15

CHAPTER 2

Technology

And knowledge shall be increased. (Dan. 12:4)

One of the many signs of the endtime is that knowledge is increased. The implication in this verse in Daniel is that this knowledge increase will be abnormal. The extraordinarily rapid growth of knowledge that we see today is a clear indication that the end of this age is approaching. This increase has become so rapid that no human can follow the advances in a single field of science, let alone throughout all its many branches. Moreover, the different branches of science are multiplying as well. Avenues of research in areas that didn't even exist twenty or thirty years ago, and weren't even contemplated fifty or sixty years ago, are now foci of intense research and development.

Nobody in biblical times could have possibly foreseen what is happening upon the earth today. Indeed, even a hundred years ago, today's exponential growth in knowledge could not have been foreseen by man. Nevertheless, as the end of days unfolds, and as the prophetic word foretold, knowledge is increasing rapidly.

The Direction of Technology

To some of us, especially those who've been observing the world situation for many years, the direction of technological advances has become increasingly clear. Astonishing developments in certain specific fields are both troubling and enlightening. What was science fiction fifty or even twenty-five years ago is now becoming science fact.

However, that science fiction was preparing the minds of the human populace to begin accepting what would once have been abhorrent and quickly rejected as unethical or immoral.

Through this subtle and even subconscious conditioning of man, new advances are often accepted with little or no questioning.

The reader may think I'm propounding some sort of conspiracy, a hidden plot to damage mankind. Truth be told, I'm proposing exactly that, for God has an enemy who has been working since the creation of man to damage and even destroy mankind. Recall the apostle John's words: "The whole world lieth in the evil one."[1]

It should come as no surprise to the Christian that Satan does have a plot—a subtle, long-term, devious plan to damage mankind to the extreme. Furthermore, to facilitate this plan he has brought forth certain scientific advances in just the right fields at the ideal time (ideal at least for his plan). While we may not clearly see what Satan's goal is with all these incredible scientific advances, there certainly is such a goal. However, as the day of the Lord's coming draws closer, what the evil one seeks is becoming more apparent. By the Lord's mercy, may we come into the light, see the truth, and be warned of the satanic trap being prepared for all mankind.

A Confluence

One thing that's striking today is the confluence of scientific advances in certain apparently disparate fields of research. That these myriad discoveries are occurring at the same time is somewhat astonishing. These developments may be buried beneath the mountain of current scientific research, but they won't escape the shining of the Spirit.

Computing

When I grew up, computing was in its infancy. When I was in college, we used slide rules[*] to do our arithmetical computations. The first pocket calculator wasn't even introduced until after I'd graduated from college. However, the last forty years have seen exponential growth in computing power, capacity, and speed, while size and cost have similarly decreased. Since the early

---

[*] Most people today don't even know what a slide rule is!

1980s, chip capacity has grown by a factor of about one billion. Processor speed has increased by a factor of about one thousand, to the threshold constraints of both manufacturing and nature's subatomic limits. Processor power has increased by a factor of perhaps one hundred thousand. Yet, cost has dropped by a factor of about one hundred billion.

Today the phones in our pockets hold subminiature processors that once would have been considered supercomputers. In fact, the current iPhone X has about twenty times the power of a 1985 Cray-2 supercomputer. Chips the size of a grain of sand are incredibly powerful—and nearly nobody is surprised. We've been conditioned!

Quantum Computing

About a decade ago, computer processors reached a kind of plateau. The circuitry in processers became so dense that it began to interfere with itself, causing malfunctions. In addition, when attempts were made to speed processors beyond a certain point, the heat generated by the circuitry running at such incredibly fast rates also caused malfunctions.* Researchers turned to other means of increasing the power of computer processors, such as increasing the number of processors running in parallel. The fact is, they ran into physical limitations that prevented them from continuing to increase computing power in the same way as they previously had.

Researchers are now pursuing possibilities in a completely new branch of science called quantum computing. While the circuitry of such computers is not inherently faster than classical computers, the processing power of these systems is exponentially greater. That is to say, far more can be done in a shorter time with a quantum computer than with a classical computer.†

---

* Currently, without employing elaborate means to cool circuitry, the fastest that processors are able to run is between four and five gigahertz (that is, between four and five billion cycles per second).

† Classical computers store and manipulate information using units called bits, which are in one of two states, typically zero or one. Quantum computers don't

Quantum computing is in its infancy, but advancing rapidly. The mathematics for quantum computation was nonexistent a few decades ago. Now quantum computers are beginning to be produced. The implications of this development are far reaching.

Artificial Intelligence

Another area that has seen astounding advances is the field of artificial intelligence (AI). What we see today in this branch of computer software wasn't possible twenty years ago. Moreover, researchers had little insight into how to develop AI software. Now, specialized circuitry called neural networks mimic the workings of the human brain, allowing an AI to learn by experience. Sophisticated AIs now develop "personalities"[*] based on the type of environment to which they're exposed, for good or for bad.[†] Advances in this field are both astonishing and deeply concerning.

Recently one engineer founded a new "religion" called Way of the Future with this stated purpose: "To develop and promote

---

have this limitation. They store and manipulate data using something called a quantum bit, or qubit. The qubit has more possible states than a simple zero or one. Its states are a combination of zero and one, something called a superposition. Because it has this far greater range of possible states and other factors, quantum computation can be far more powerful and informative in certain situations. However, there's a catch—these other, nonclassical states of qubits are not directly accessible. They exist but cannot be directly measured. Consequently, stored data in qubits has to be manipulated in such a way as to enable extraction of the particular piece of information wanted. For this reason, special algorithms have to be devised for quantum computers. As a consequence, only certain types of problems lend themselves to quantum computing and to the vast increase in power it provides. Classical computer algorithms would run no faster on a quantum computer than on a classical one.

[*] This is not to say that these AIs have a person, a consciousness, or an awareness in the human sense. By referring to an AI's "personality," I mean the *appearance* of a personality. There are already computer programs that can so accurately mimic human responses that they appear to have a human personality. It should be understood throughout this book that I don't mean to imply that AIs have or will have actual consciousness. Rather, they're simply sophisticated machines that may appear to have consciousness.

[†] Indeed, a recent AI (called "Norman") created at MIT demonstrated a psychopathic "personality" after being exposed to data about gruesome deaths.

the realization of a Godhead based on artificial intelligence, and through understanding and worship of the Godhead contribute to the betterment of society." Its undertakings will center on "the realization, acceptance, and worship of a Godhead based on Artificial Intelligence (AI) developed through computer hardware and software." Such an AI—one that's perhaps a billion times smarter than the most intelligent human being—is predicted to emerge within the next twenty-five years.

Virtual Reality

For some years, computers have had the power and capability to broadcast entire environments to a user's display or other optical device. As computers have increased in power and computer software has become more sophisticated, the virtual reality (VR) environments produced by them have greatly increased in resolution and become more feature-rich and realistic.

Augmented reality combines computer-generated sensory information (visual, audial, haptic, etc.) with the real-world environment. The blending of the digital augmentation with the surrounding environment can be so realistic that the augmentation is perceived to be part of that environment.

MMOs

Massively multiplayer online games (MMOGs, or simply MMOs) allow hundreds or thousands of individuals, located in diverse locations, to share the same VR environment hosted by the same computer server. In this environment, individuals can interact with each other as well as with the virtual environment surrounding them.

Exoskeletons

Exoskeletons are external, wearable, rigid or semi-rigid frames with powered motors and other mechanical devices that augment the wearer's natural abilities. In military applications such suits provide increased speed, strength, and endurance. Exoskeletons are already being tested and deployed in certain armies.

Future versions of such enhancements may well provide superhuman strength, agility, and speed.

Robotics

The field of robotics has advanced literally by leaps and bounds. By doing a simple internet search, one can find videos of newly developed robots that leap and do somersaults. Viewers of such feats comment about how frightening these robots are.

Communications

The speed and clarity at which communications networks currently operate is staggering. Communications that once required a wired connection are now done wirelessly. Cellular connections can exceed 80 megabits per second. This is astounding, and it's only a 4G network. The next generation of cellular communications, 5G, should begin being deployed this year. It will allow the download of a two-hour 4K movie (about 100 gigabytes in size) in less than four minutes. The 5G standard will allow transfer rates of about four gigabits per second.

In a very short time, virtually anything stored digitally on the whole planet will be accessible nearly instantaneously. Already, multiplayer VR games, in which the participants are networked together over the internet and share a VR that's at least partially streamed (i.e., transmitted) to them live, have been available for quite some time. A complete VR environment will soon be streamable to anyone who wants it.

Thirty years ago, I read books that spoke of such virtual reality environments in the distant future—hundreds or even thousands of years from now. This is science fiction becoming science fact.

Neural Implants

Finally, there's one more technology that must be mentioned, for it may well play a prominent role during the endtime. Researchers and physicians have been experimenting for some time with the direct connection of circuitry to living tissue, and have enjoyed great success.

More recently they've turned their attention to the direct connection to the brain. Recent experiments have demonstrated such connections to the brains of rats, with functioning circuitry not only communicating to their brains but even allowing an electronic connection between the brains of different rats.

Extensive research and experimentation with human brains is ongoing. Neural implants (computer chips implanted upon the brain) are currently in use. Some are attempting to help those with disabilities. Others are attempting to augment the brain's functions, such as by enhancing memory.

In the somewhat near future, such chips are expected to extend the dynamic range of the senses and enable what is called cyberthink—invisible, wireless, brain-to-brain communication between humans. A recent startup called Neuralink aims to build a brain-computer interface allowing a direct connection between the internet and the human brain. The consequences of such developments are intensely disturbing, as we'll see.

The Overlord

Many shall run to and fro, and knowledge shall be increased. (Dan. 12:4)

Daniel 12:4 also mentions that many will run to and fro. Some liken this to today's automobile traffic. However, that's not the point of this verse. Rather, it's speaking about the frenetic pace at which mankind will be driven as his knowledge is greatly increased.

In the time of Moses, Pharaoh and his Egyptian taskmasters enslaved the Hebrews and drove them mercilessly and incessantly to build store-cities. Today it's the same, yet on a much grander scale and with much deeper spiritual implications. Today, Satan has enslaved all mankind. He has enslaved man with greed and lust. To trap and enslave humanity, Satan uses greed for money and material possessions, as well as lust for power, fame, or sex.

Man is caught in the satanic web of a brutal taskmaster, and for the most part—like one wandering in a drug-induced dream state—the captive is nearly completely unaware of his dire plight.

Satan is mercilessly driving the entire human race to work at an ever faster and more intense rate. Mankind is blindly rushing headlong, in a frenzy of activity, to create and build one final great "monument" to the evil one, not knowing that this will bring about mankind's own demise. Using his sin-filled opiates* as enticements, Satan has accelerated man's pace to an incredible level. People are working sixty, eighty, or even more hours a week as their managers demand more, and as Satan and his taskmasters require more from the managers. What is Satan doing? He has his goal, his final and greatest accomplishment. He's lashing and driving mankind to produce it, all the while supplying the necessary scientific advancements† for its construction.

References

[1] 1 Jn. 5:19

---

* That is, material wealth, power, sex, and the like.

† Just as Pharaoh supplied straw to the Hebrews.

CHAPTER 3

The Abomination Revealed

As the end approaches, one technology after another will mature, all in a timely fashion, for Satan's last great effort to thwart God's move on the earth. Computer-generated VR environments, as well as augmented-reality environments, will become indistinguishable from actuality. Lifelike robots that mimic the actions of human beings will be developed. Importantly, functioning quantum computers will come into being. These will have sufficient reliable qubits to make them many orders of magnitude more powerful[*] than classical computers. Along with the development of quantum computers, specialized algorithms tailored to these processers will be developed in fields such as meteorology, cryptanalysis, and game theory, especially when applied to military situations.

The Beast and the AI Deity

And the king shall do according to his will; and he shall exalt himself, and magnify himself above every god, and shall speak marvellous things against the God of gods; and he shall prosper till the indignation be accomplished; for that which is determined shall be done. Neither shall he regard the gods of his fathers, nor the desire of women, nor regard any god; for he shall magnify himself above all. But in his place shall he honor the god of fortresses; and a god whom his fathers knew not shall he honor with gold, and silver, and with precious stones and pleasant things. And he shall deal with the strongest fortresses by the help of a

---

[*] A processor with 49 qubits is thought to be more powerful than all the world's supercomputers combined, a threshold called quantum supremacy. Google recently announced a 72-qubit processor. However, it will be some time before these experimental machines are commercially viable.

foreign god: whosoever acknowledgeth him he will increase with glory; and he shall cause them to rule over many, and shall divide the land for a price. (Dan. 11:36-39)

Mankind's "crowning" achievement—for which Satan has driven man these many decades—will be an artificial intelligence "god." When this is developed, it will fall into the hands of the beast, the Antichrist.

The beast will be godless. He won't care for any religion or any religion's god, whether Christian, Muslim, or of some other religion. He will not regard the gods of his fathers. While essentially godless, the Antichrist will greatly value and revere the AI "deity."

The beast will use the enormous capabilities of this AI to wage war. As he fights, city after city and stronghold after stronghold will fall before him due to AI-developed strategies. No one will be able to stand against him and his onslaught as he sweeps across Eastern Europe, North Africa, and Israel.[1]

This AI will be vastly more intelligent than any human being, perhaps a million or a billion times so. There will be no comparison between its strategies and tactics and those of the military computers and strategists of its foes.

It will have at its disposal multiple quantum computers that are each many orders of magnitude more powerful than any classical computer ever produced. Sophisticated software algorithms devised solely to wage war in any and all conditions and circumstances will be developed* along with the quantum computers. No one will be able to stand before the beast and the god who helps him.

The beast will not only honor this artificial intelligence, but treat it as a god. The AI deity will seem to know everything, be able to solve any problem, overcome every difficulty. It will become the god of the godless Antichrist.

With the assistance of the AI deity in his possession, the European leader will seem invincible. The enormous intellectual power provided by this computer, with its tactical and strategic

---

* The AI deity may actually develop the software itself.

decision-making capabilities, will provide such a huge advantage to the beast that no one will be able to overcome him.

It may be that this great European leader comes into possession of this artificial intelligence even before he rises to power. And it may be through the AI's assistance that the Antichrist rises from obscurity to become emperor. We simply don't know how much of the Antichrist's acumen, intelligence, and seeming genius is due to his own capabilities and how much to those of a super-minded artificial intelligence.

Consider the resources that will be available to the Antichrist with such a computer. All of the internet, with all of mankind's history, will be accessible virtually instantaneously to the AI to be used in its decision-making and recommendations to the Antichrist. Furthermore, everything connected to the internet will become available for the AI's use—including commercial and personal security cameras, other computers attached to the internet, and home devices with an internet connection.

By that time, who can say how much of the lives of the earth's people will be monitored by one device or another that's internet-linked. This AI will have so much capability and power that it will be able to access everything, surreptitiously breaking through any firewall or other computer defense. Like an insidious virus, it will take over the whole internet.

With such surveillance capabilities at his disposal, the Antichrist will be able to easily defeat any challenger or enemy. He'll know beforehand what his foes plan to do. With his AI deity's help, planning a response to such attacks will be child's play for the Antichrist. No one on earth will be able to stop him.

It would seem that the Antichrist's AI deity will be unique, or at least considerably more powerful than any other AI in existence. Otherwise, why wouldn't the Antichrist's strategies, tactics, plans, and plots be thwarted by opposing AIs? In some way the Antichrist will be able to neutralize all competition, including that in the digital realm.

With this understanding of the Antichrist's AI deity, we can now explain the mystery in Daniel 11:36-39. With respect to all the gods of those who've gone before him, the Antichrist will have no regard whatsoever—he'll be godless. He'll worship no god in the sense of what men now consider to be a god. But he'll revere a machine with its sophisticated man-made software AI. This, to the Antichrist, will be a god, although it was unknown to his forefathers. Futhermore, this "foreign god" will assist him in overthrowing all strongholds that stand in his way. It will be the god of strongholds.

The Image of the Beast

And he deceiveth them that dwell on the earth by reason of the signs which it was given him to do in the sight of the beast; saying to them that dwell on the earth, that they should make an image to the beast who hath the stroke of the sword and lived. And it was given unto him to give breath to it, even to the image of the beast, that the image of the beast should both speak, and cause that as many as should not worship the image of the beast should be killed. (Rev. 13:14-15)

But when ye see the abomination of desolation standing where he ought not (let him that readeth understand), then let them that are in Judæa flee unto the mountains. (Matt. 24:15)

    The second piece of the endtime puzzle concerns the image of the beast that will be set up by the false prophet. It's clear that this will be no ordinary image. It will be able to speak and to cause those not worshiping it to be killed. Based upon the direction of current technology and its increasingly rapid growth, this image may be an AI-endowed android.[*] This AI should be the same one[†] that the Antichrist will use to conquer his enemies and maintain his control.

    As mentioned in chapter 2, the possibility has been demonstrated for developing an AI with a psychopathic personality by subjecting it to information detailing gruesome deaths. Suppose an AI were fed information about Satan, satanic worship, and evil

---

[*] That is, a robot with a human outward appearance.

[†] Given how processing is distributed among many thousands of computers at the current time, it should not be considered strange that the AI deity could be functioning in many places through many devices simultaneously. In effect, it may appear to be omnipresent among men.

deeds of all kinds—such as Hitler's reign in Germany. What kind of personality would it develop? I conjecture that it would develop a devilish personality. Furthermore, based upon the behavior of the image of the beast as described in Revelation 13, it would seem that this image has just such a character. It is self-exalting and "wanting" to be worshiped, just like Satan. It seeks to compel others to its own will—also like Satan. Finally, it is murderous, like the one who was a murderer from the beginning.² In short, the image of the beast is Satan in machine form.*

It's likely that the image of the beast will be a murderous and devilish AI with extraordinary capabilities contained within an android body. Such an understanding lends new meaning to the Lord's word in Matthew 24:15. The image is standing not as something placed there, but as a man stands because he chooses to do so.

Taking technology into account, it's again simple to understand what once were conundrums in the Bible regarding the beast and those things that relate to him. The image speaks because it's an AI-invested computer and has been given the man-made capacity to speak. It seeks to compel others to worship it, and kills those who don't because it purposely has a devilish personality in order to express Satan. It's an abomination because it has no life, no soul, and no actual awareness, though it behaves as if it does. It's something God sees as beyond despicable—it is an abomination.

---

* In Gen. 6:2, the sons of God (i.e., fallen angels) took human form and mingled themselves with mankind. God judged that wicked age by the flood in Noah's day. Everyone except Noah and his family was destroyed by that flood, including those angels who had taken human form. These were cast down into Tarturus to pits of darkness to await judgment (2 Pet. 2:4). God would not tolerate angels leaving their station.

Satan is too intelligent to make such a mistake and allow himself to be quickly judged by God and so easily defeated. Rather than take human form himself, he will bring forth an AI with the capability to largely match his own extraordinary intelligence. He'll invest this AI with his own devilish character. Through the Antichrist and the AI diety, Satan will be able to fully manifest himself and interact with man without the danger of taking human form. It may also be that Satan will directly control, adjust, or in some other way influence the decision-making process of the AI. No doubt he considers this a brilliant strategy on his part, not believing that his end is already determined.

The Mark of the Beast

The final piece of this puzzle concerns the mark of the beast. What is so extraordinary about a mark in the skin on the forehead or hand? Why would such a mark be so important? While it's true that it designates the bearer as one who belongs to the Antichrist and to his image, I believe there's much more to this mark—something far more insidious.

It's possible that this mark is not merely a number or a name imprinted on the flesh, but rather some sort of access port or communications node to connect the AI deity directly to the brain through a cerebral implant. This is certainly the direction of today's technology.

Consider the ramifications of such a direct cerebral link to an artificial intelligence. The AI would be able to stream whatever VR or perceptual augmentations it chooses to those who have the mark of the beast. With such a direct link to the brains of the Antichrist's followers, it might be able to substitute its own virtual reality for the real world. Those who've given themselves over to such an abominable modification will be totally under the control of a devilish AI. They'll think they can trust this incredibly intelligent machine, not knowing that their entire experience is a lie being injected into their brains by a satanic personality.

With its direct links to those bearing the mark of the beast, to the internet, and to peripheral devices that are internet-linked, the AI will be able to pass on whatever information it chooses to any of the Antichrist's followers nearly instantaneously. It will know the whereabouts of almost everyone, including those Jews sealed in Revelation 7 and moving throughout Israel to preach the gospel of the kingdom and testify concerning Jesus. This means that it can direct one or more of those with the mark to any spot, to wherever it wants them to be, to carry out the devilish and murderous plans it has devised.

Delusion

And another angel, a third, followed them, saying with a great voice, If any man worshippeth the beast and his image, and receiveth a mark on his forehead, or upon his hand, he also shall drink of the wine of the wrath of God, which is prepared unmixed in the cup of his anger; and he shall be tormented with fire and brimstone in the presence of the holy angels, and in the presence of the Lamb: and the smoke of their torment goeth up for ever and ever; and they have no rest day and night, they that worship the beast and his image, and whoso receiveth the mark of his name. (Rev. 14:9-11)

And the first went, and poured out his bowl into the earth; and it became a noisome and grievous sore upon the men that had the mark of the beast, and that worshipped his image.... And the fourth poured out his bowl upon the sun; and it was given unto it to scorch men with fire. And men were scorched with great heat: and they blasphemed the name of God who hath the power over these plagues; and they repented not to give him glory. And the fifth poured out his bowl upon the throne of the beast; and his kingdom was darkened; and they gnawed their tongues for pain, and they blasphemed the God of heaven because of their pains and their sores; and they repented not of their works. (Rev. 16:2, 8-10)

In Revelation 14 there's a warning not to receive the mark of the beast; those who do will suffer the judgment of fire eternally. However, in Revelation 16, the bowls are poured out upon the beast's kingdom and specifically upon those who have his mark and worship his image. However, as these verses mention, this is done in the hope that somehow those with the mark can be brought to repentance. If they're destined for eternal fire, why is God still trying to bring them to repentance? God's heart is to somehow save them in any way possible, yet the ones with the mark have become so damaged that there's no possibility of their receiving such a salvation. Why?

So many human beings suffer from psychological problems of various kinds. Many of these troubles essentially stem from a deeply held belief in something that isn't true. In our lives, over time, we may construct upon such untruths an elaborate inward psychological edifice. Such personality problems can cause enormous difficulties in one's daily life, in human relationships, in the perception of surrounding events, and especially in the perception of one's self. For the Christian, it can cause serious problems in seeking and experiencing Christ. These inward issues become huge obstacles to normal living, especially for a proper Christian life.

This kind of condition might begin (and perhaps usually does) with something real and genuine, something that isn't a lie. It may be traumatic, like abuse of some kind. Or it could be something overly pleasant, like being doted upon continually. Whatever the case, if the improper environment isn't remedied, over time the human psyche will increasingly perceive what is improper as being normal and common.

For example, if we've suffered abuse and traumatic treatment, this can leave a lasting and even indelible impression upon us, especially if such abuse occurs over a long period of time. We then feel and sense such abuse around us and toward us unconsciously, even when it isn't present.

At the other extreme, if we've always been treated in a special way, handled daintily, or allowed to do as we please, then over time within ourselves we become accustomed to that impropriety. Unconsciously we start believing that the universe revolves around us, that we're something special and deserve special treatment.

If this condition isn't treated, it not only remains but grows. We begin to live in a kind of fantasy. Whether our fantasy is a delightful fairytale or a horrible nightmare, it's still a fantasy—something unreal. Day by day we're living inwardly in an unreal psychological world.

This condition can worsen over time. It can become severe enough to develop into a delusion. When we live in a fantasy, we're still able—given proper guidance—to discern what's real and what isn't when confronted with certain facts and events. When our condition has worsened into a delusion, we believe that inward fantasy realm to be true no matter what facts dispute our belief. We cannot be convinced that it's untrue. When confronted with something contrary to our delusion, we ignore or twist facts in order to maintain our delusional state. What is delusion? It is deception incorporated into our being at a fundamental level.

It may be that every person on earth suffers from this kind of problem to one degree or another. Becoming a Christian, being born again, does not automatically save us from such a state and its accompanying problems.

God loves mankind. He loves both believers and unbelievers. He sees that these kinds of psychological problems, if left unchecked, will severely and perhaps irreparably damage us. And so He intervenes. He arranges certain events, certain happenings in our lives to help treat our condition, to awaken us from our fantasies, and in severe cases to end the delusions. God uses quite a variety of difficulties in our lives to help save us from our condition. God will try again and again to rescue us from fantasy and delusion and deliver us into reality. His dealings in this regard begin gently. But over time, if we disregard the healing treatment being offered to us, His dealings may become stronger, harder, and harsher. He will try in every way possible to cure us from our debilitating disease.

As an example, consider Job in the Old Testament. Most people consider the book of Job to be a story about God testing a man's patience. You've certainly heard of "the patience of Job." However, this is absolutely wrong! The book of Job is not about a man's patience. This is the perception of those who haven't seen that Job was diseased. What was his disease? He considered himself righteous. He was self-righteous to the point of being delusional. The book of Job is about delusion and about the extremes to which God will go to save one He loves from that great deception.

If you look carefully at Job's words throughout that whole book, you'll see something striking: he always believed he was right. He always maintained he'd done nothing wrong. He was so strong in this belief that he'd become delusional. What's worse, that delusion was keeping him from God. Job was locked in himself, in his self-righteous and delusional self. It wasn't possible for him to see beyond what he was.

So God allowed Satan to torment Job in various ways. First, Satan destroyed his possessions and killed his servants and his sons and daughters.[3] But Job held fast his integrity.[4] God then allowed Satan to touch his flesh with painful boils from head to foot.[5] But Job still held fast.[6]

As these treatments came Job's way, he refused to let go of his delusion of self-righteousness. In each case, he maintained his integrity, holding fast to his own righteousness. He refused to let go of his delusion. He really believed he was righteous in every way and without fault. This not only prevented him from seeing his own true condition; more importantly, it kept him from seeing and knowing God.

It wasn't until the end of the book, after Job had been thoroughly broken down by all that had come upon him, that Job finally saw.[7] And when he did, he abhorred himself.[8] He saw what he really was and how he had been all along. He finally saw both his true condition and God Himself. It took all that Job passed through to save him from his delusion.

Now consider those who receive the mark of the beast. They'll certainly be delusional even before they receive the mark. They'll believe there's no God, they'll worship a machine, and they'll be willing to have implants inserted into their brains so they can communicate directly with this machine. They're not simply delusional. They're possessed by their delusion.

In their case, their delusional state will be constantly and continually reinforced, moment by moment, by a devilish AI through the virtual and false reality being streamed to them through their cerebral connection to it. The plagues God sends upon them throughout the last three and a half years by the two witnesses, Moses and Elijah, are not to torment them, but are rather the divine attempt to wake them from the falsehood of the delusion in which they live.

Eventually, the last plagues—the seven bowls—are God's ultimate attempt to bring them to repentance and rescue them from their delusion. Unfortunately, their direct machine-to-mind connection to the Antichrist's AI will damage them beyond repair. They won't turn from their delusion. Nothing will remain except to cast them into the lake of fire. For this reason, God sends an angel[9] at the beginning of the last three and a half years to warn all men not to receive the mark of the beast, telling them that those who do will end up in eternal fire.

The Abomination of Desolation

...they shall set up the abomination that maketh desolate. (Dan. 11:31)

When therefore ye see the abomination of desolation, which was spoken of through Daniel the prophet, standing in the holy place... (Matt. 24:15)

The image of the Antichrist with its artificial intelligence is called an abomination. To understand why, we simply need to look closely at what it is.

First, it's a machine and nothing more. It has a character—a devilish personality—imprinted upon its neural network, but it has no life. It has no personhood, no soul, no conscience, no consciousness, not even awareness (at least in the human sense of the word). While it has the appearance of all these, in fact it's nothing but a very sophisticated machine.

Second, the "personality" with which it has been endowed is deceitful, murderous, evil, devilish. It will be trained and will develop by observing things that are deceitful and evil. As the machine-expression of Satan himself, it will have no regard for God, no empathy or concern for others. Its programming will place itself first in all circumstances.

Third, it will control human beings. This machine that has no will, no soul, no conscience, no spirit, and no life will control living human beings. It will be Satan "incarnate," without having Satan within. It will be a true abomination, a diabolical mixture of synthetic intelligence and electronic circuitry.

Furthermore, it will be fixated upon destruction—destroying men, destroying nations, destroying the earth. Whatever it touches will suffer destruction. Just as Satan (its source) is—so will it be. The malice of that evil angel will be reflected in this vile machine. It will be focused on but one thing: devastation, primarily of the Jews. It will not be just an abomination, but an abomination of destruction—the abomination of desolation.

The Abomination of the Mark

And another angel, a third, followed them, saying with a great voice, If any man worshippeth the beast and his image, and receiveth a mark on his forehead, or upon his hand, he also shall drink of the wine of the wrath of God, which is prepared unmixed in the cup of his anger; and he shall be tormented with fire and brimstone in the presence of the holy angels, and in the presence of the Lamb: and the smoke of their torment goeth up for ever and ever; and they have no rest day and night, they that worship the beast and his image, and whoso receiveth the mark of his name. (Rev. 14:9-11)

Those who receive the mark of the beast will be a kind of hybrid, part human and part machine. The mark's neural implants will connect them directly to the synthetic intelligence of the Antichrist's AI deity. Essentially they'll become cyborgs—part human, part machine.* They'll be heavily influenced and perhaps even completely controlled by a computer superintelligence. What's worse, that synthetic mind directing them will be devilish, an electronic replica of the evil one. They'll become extensions of this machine, and in effect human extensions of Satan himself.

Those who receive this neural implant will also be abominations. Not only will they be perverted physically, but their psychology, their soul, will be warped irreparably by the interaction with this fiendish AI. This direct AI-human communication within a person's brain at such a deep level will do something unimaginable to them. Their perceptions and inward experience will become something nonhuman, something inhuman. They, too, will be abominations at all levels—physically, psychologically, and spiritually.

Unable to turn from the satanic deception of their delusion and unwilling to forsake the fantastical lie being injected into them by the AI, those with the mark of the beast will suffer endlessly in the lake of fire. They'll follow their leaders, the two beasts—the Antichrist and the false prophet—into perdition.

The Abomination of the Beast

In addition, consider the beast, the Antichrist. He'll be merely human as he rises to power, although during this period he'll be aided spiritually by Satan, and aided materially by a devilish AI. He'll be slain in the middle of the last seven years, then resuscitated by the spirit of Caesar Nero.

---

* Such "cyborgs" are already beginning to appear.

What kind of being will he then be? How can such a monstrous thing be described? The body of one human will be inhabited by the spirit of another. What is this? This is yet another abomination. Everything to do with the Antichrist during the endtime will be an abomination—abomination upon abomination.

The Great Counterfeit

And I saw, and behold, the Lamb standing on the mount Zion, and with him a hundred and forty and four thousand, having his name, and the name of his Father, written on their foreheads. And I heard a voice from heaven, as the voice of many waters, and as the voice of a great thunder: and the voice which I heard was as the voice of harpers harping with their harps: and they sing as it were a new song before the throne, and before the four living creatures and the elders: and no man could learn the song save the hundred and forty and four thousand, even they that had been purchased out of the earth. These are they that were not defiled with women; for they are virgins. These are they that follow the Lamb whithersoever he goeth. These were purchased from among men, to be the firstfruits unto God and unto the Lamb. And in their mouth was found no lie: they are without blemish. (Rev. 14:1-5)

And I saw a beast coming up out of the sea, having ten horns and seven heads, and on his horns ten diadems, and upon his heads names of blasphemy.... And it was given unto him to give breath to it, even to the image of the beast, that the image of the beast should both speak, and cause that as many as should not worship the image of the beast should be killed. And he causeth all, the small and the great, and the rich and the poor, and the free and the bond, that there be given them a mark on their right hand, or upon their forehead; and that no man should be able to buy or to sell, save he that hath the mark, even the name of the beast or the number of his name. (Rev. 13:1, 15-17)

In the first book of this series, we saw the beautiful scene on the heavenly Mount Zion at the beginning of the last three and a half years of this age. God the Father will be there on the throne. Before Him will be the indescribable Jesus. With Jesus will be the many groups of mature believers who've been blessed with that breathtaking and transcendent state of being. All the New Testament martyrs will be there as well, a reward for their having given their lives for the Lord.

The Father will pour out life to all, commanding His promised blessing.[10] Believers will rejoice in this blessing, as they're led[11] in song by the wonderful Spirit of God. Most glorious of all will be the incomparable Jesus.[12] This will be the dispensational fulfillment of God's desire and plan from eternity—many men lifted from the earth to the level of divinity to be God's sons before Him in love,[13] sharing and participating in all He is and does. Everything here will be in oneness, through fellowship, and in love. What a sweet and pleasant scene!

These verses in Revelation 14 are a direct continuation of Revelation 12:12. If you omit the intervening verses (from 12:13 to 13:18), you'll see that this is one continuous vision of the heavenly scene. The end of chapter 12 and all of chapter 13 read as if they're an insertion. Why are these verses placed here between Revelation 12 and 14? What is God trying to show us by this?

Chapter 13 is juxtaposed to the beginning of Revelation 14. While God is enjoying the mature believers in the heavens, Satan will be bringing about his counterfeit on the earth. As always, he'll mimic what God has done, but in a perverted and twisted way. He'll rule over men as a self-enthroned king through an AI replica of himself. But he does not bless, as God does; rather, he coerces, deceives, and bribes men to follow him. And instead of a breathtakingly beautiful Christ at the fore, Satan will have a beast, the Antichrist, as leader. He'll be a monstrosity. The Antichrist will be as foul as Christ is beautiful.

Finally, instead of men who've been brought up to the level of divinity by God the Spirit working within them, there'll be those with the mark of the beast. Those on the heavenly Mount Zion have the name of God and the Lamb on their foreheads. The beast's followers have the number or the name of the beast on theirs. Instead of being raised to the highest point possible, they've been lowered to humanity's deepest pit.

They're machine controlled and machine driven; they're soulless and heartless automatons of a terrible sort. Worse than any worshipers of false gods throughout time, they will not simply worship a machine, but become physically one with it. Instead of life flowing to them, they'll experience the devilish, machine-originated, perception-changing, deceiving and coercing instructions, commandments, and delusion-inducing data from a lifeless machine. This is Satan's great counterfeit, which he's driving man toward in the pursuit of scientific and technological knowledge.

This is why Revelation 13 is placed between 12 and 14. God is presenting us with a stark contrast between His achievement in man and Satan's—between man lifted to the heavens and man brought down to the most miserable condition in the lowest pit.

God is presenting man with a choice, one that has been before man's eyes for almost two millennia: Will you follow Christ to reach the transcendent peak of Mount Zion? Or will you give yourself over to the evil one and his deceptions, becoming so corrupted, damaged, and fouled that you follow him into his destiny of eternal fire?

What a clear and stark choice!

References

[1] Dan. 8:9
[2] John 8:44
[3] Job. 1:13-19
[4] Job 2:3
[5] Job 2:7
[6] Job 2:10
[7] Job 42:5
[8] Job 42:6
[9] Rev. 14:9-11
[10] Psa. 133:1-3
[11] Rom. 8:14
[12] Rev. 14:1
[13] Eph. 1:3-6

CHAPTER 4

The Darkest Time

The middle of Daniel's seventieth week will be an earth-shattering time. Numerous events will occur nearly simultaneously that will reshape the world. These, coupled with the events at the end of the age immediately preceding the Lord's physical return, will completely remake the earth to prepare it for the millennial kingdom.

At the halfway juncture of the last seven years, there will be a great nexus of events. The many things that happen will bring about enormous changes in a very brief period of time, perhaps no more than a few days. These will set the stage for the last three and a half years before the Lord's second coming. Those few days will be momentous.

The Rapture

Then shall two men be in the field; one is taken, and one is left: two women shall be grinding at the mill; one is taken, and one is left. Watch therefore: for ye know not on what day your Lord cometh. (Matt. 24:40-42)

But of that day and hour knoweth no one, not even the angels of heaven, neither the Son, but the Father only. (Matt. 24:36)

Sometime before the last three and a half years, the mature saints will be taken from the earth. All who are ready will be taken; all who are not ready will be left. We will not know beforehand when this will happen; we won't know until the moment occurs. That time is hidden in the Father.

Shortly after this, the martyred New Testament saints—the manchild of Revelation 12—will be resurrected and also caught up to God's throne. They'll take command of God's angelic army and command it to cast Satan and his angels from the heavens.

The Sixth Seal

They ate, they drank, they married, they were given in marriage, until the day that Noah entered into the ark, and the flood came, and destroyed them all. (Luke 17:27)

Once the mature believers are removed from the earth, God's judgment upon the earth will commence. Recall the Lord's word: the day that Noah entered the ark, the flood came. So it will be at the end of this age. Christ will open the sixth seal and the events pictured in Revelation 6^1 and in Joel 2^2 will occur.* The whole earth will be shaken by this occurrence, but it will merely be a harbinger of what's to come—something far worse.

The Two Witnesses

And I will give unto my two witnesses, and they shall prophesy a thousand two hundred and threescore days, clothed in sackcloth. These are the two olive trees and the two candlesticks, standing before the Lord of the earth. (Rev. 11:3-4)

Moses and Elijah will then appear in Israel. As the Law and the Prophets in the Old Testament testify of Christ, so Moses the lawgiver and Elijah the prophet will testify of Christ in Israel during the last three and a half years. They should also instruct, train, and direct those Jews who will be sealed by God and who will carry the testimony of Jesus to the cities of Israel.

The 144,000 of Israel

And it shall come to pass afterward, that I will pour out my Spirit upon all flesh; and your sons and your daughters shall prophesy, your old men shall dream dreams, your young men shall see visions: and also upon the servants and upon the handmaids in those days will I pour out my Spirit. And I will show wonders in the heavens and in the earth: blood, and fire, and pillars of smoke. The sun shall be turned into darkness, and the moon into blood,

---

* Revelation 6:12-14 and Joel 2:30-31 actually refer to the same event. The record in Revelation is from a global perspective; that in Joel is from the perspective of Israel.

before the great and terrible day of Jehovah cometh. And it shall come to pass, that whosoever shall call on the name of Jehovah shall be delivered. (Joel 2:28-32)

The events that accompany the opening of the sixth seal will shake the earth. However, as depicted in Joel, they'll also serve as a sign to many of the Jews. At this time, 144,000 of Israel will be sealed by God. They'll be instructed to wait for the abomination of desolation to stand in the temple. They're to then flee to the mountains, where they'll be kept from the terrible torment that will occur in Israel. At the same time, they'll be instructed by Moses and Elijah regarding their testimony throughout Israel.

The Antichrist Slain

And I saw one of his heads as though it had been smitten unto death... (Rev. 13:3)

By this time, the Antichrist should be dead, slain by the sword. This may well occur in Israel, as the Jews gather to commemorate the completion of the rebuilding of the temple. Most of the people of the Antichrist's ten-nation empire will mourn and lament him, weeping over his loss. Their great leader will be gone.

The Flood of Judgment

And when he opened the seventh seal, there followed a silence in heaven about the space of half an hour. And I saw the seven angels that stand before God; and there were given unto them seven trumpets. And another angel came and stood over the altar, having a golden censer; and there was given unto him much incense, that he should add it unto the prayers of all the saints upon the golden altar which was before the throne. And the smoke of the incense, with the prayers of the saints, went up before God out of the angel's hand. And the angel taketh the censer; and he filled it with the fire of the altar, and cast it upon the earth: and there followed thunders, and voices, and lightnings, and an earthquake. And the seven angels that had the seven trumpets prepared themselves to sound. And the first sounded, and there followed hail and fire, mingled with blood, and they were cast upon the earth: and the third part of the earth was burnt up, and the third part of the trees was burnt up, and all green grass was burnt up. And the second angel sounded, and as it were a great mountain burning with fire was cast into the sea: and the third part of the sea became blood; and there died the third part of the creatures which were in the sea, even they that had life; and the third part of the ships was destroyed. And the third angel sounded, and there fell from heaven a great star, burning as a torch, and it fell upon the third part of the rivers, and upon the fountains of the waters; and the name of the star is called Wormwood: and the third part of the waters became wormwood; and many men died of the waters, because they were made bitter. And the fourth angel sounded, and the third part of the sun was smitten, and the third part of the moon, and the third part of the stars; that the third part of them should be darkened, and the day should not shine for the third part of it, and the night in like manner. (Rev. 8:1-12)

God will then severely judge the earth by the seventh seal and the first four trumpets. The earth will be left nearly totally destroyed. While there may be small pockets of lesser damage, the earth as we know it today will on the whole be gone. All of Asia will be in ruins; the whole Pacific rim will be obliterated; the southern Atlantic and Atlantic coasts will suffer enormous damage; nor will southern Africa, northern Australia, and the islands of the Pacific escape this destruction.

The one area that will pass through this time relatively unscathed will be around the Mediterranean—southern Europe, the Middle East, and northern Africa. These must remain intact for the fulfillment of prophecy, for the continuation of the Antichrist's empire until the Lord's return, and so that Israel might repent and be saved at the end of the age.

By these judgments the whole world order will be upended. The United States will be brought to her knees. China will be decimated, along with Russia. The great world powers will be gone.

In addition, in the aftermath of these judgments, the earth's surface temperature will fall due to the enormous amount of airborne debris blocking sunlight, making the more northerly latitudes virtually uninhabitable. Canada, Siberia, northern Europe, Greenland, and other northerly locations will become desolate until the earth recovers from God's judgments.

Through these events, the earth will be brought back to the state it was two thousand years ago. Rome, the capital of the revived Roman Empire, along with the rest of the area around the Mediterranean will once again be the center of the inhabited earth.

In only a few days, God will change everything.*

The Abyss

I saw a star from heaven fallen unto the earth: and there was given to him the key of the pit of the abyss. And he opened the pit of the abyss; and there went up a smoke out of the pit, as the smoke of a great furnace; and the sun and the air were darkened by reason of the smoke of the pit. And out of the smoke came forth locusts upon the earth; and power was given them, as the scorpions of the earth have power. (Rev. 9:1-3)

The earth will be in unprecedented chaos and nearly totally destroyed. The intensity and scope on this disaster will be unprecedented. In the midst of this storm, the area around the Mediterranean will be a place of relative calm, like the eye of a hurricane.

Having been cast to the earth, Satan will stand upon the Mediterranean shore and open the shaft of the abyss. He'll release a swarm of "locusts." In addition, he'll release their king, Abaddon.

As we've already seen, Abaddon refers to the spirit of Caesar Nero. Similarly, the locusts do not refer to some sort of gruesome insect. Rather, these are also spirits, the spirits of demons bound in the abyss until just this moment.

The spirit of Nero will inhabit the dead corpse of the Antichrist, resuscitating him and apparently resurrecting him from the dead miraculously. The demons will inhabit the bodies of the Antichrist's army, turning them into a horde of demon-possessed soldiers, seemingly unstoppable and particularly vicious.

---

* There's one very important side effect to all these events. Technology being produced anywhere other then Europe and the Middle East will be destroyed. Only the technology in the Antichrist's empire will remain. *There will be no competitors for the Antichrist's AI deity.*

Consolidating Power

A time of unknown duration will ensue, during which the resuscitated Antichrist, his army, and his followers will deal with the upheaval in Europe that will be caused by the great destruction around the earth. There will be countless acute problems produced by God's judgments upon earth. Every link from the Antichrist's empire to the rest of the world will have been severed. Banking systems will be totally disrupted. Foreign suppliers of raw material and goods to Europe will have ceased operations. All modes of transportation will have been interrupted. Overseas communications will be nonexistent, at least temporarily. It will take some time for these problems to be properly managed and for the Antichrist to consolidate power.

The Second Beast

And I saw another beast coming up out of the earth; and he had two horns like unto a lamb, and he spake as a dragon. And he exerciseth all the authority of the first beast in his sight. And he maketh the earth and them that dwell therein to worship the first beast, whose death-stroke was healed. And he doeth great signs, that he should even make fire to come down out of heaven upon the earth in the sight of men. And he deceiveth them that dwell on the earth by reason of the signs which it was given him to do in the sight of the beast; saying to them that dwell on the earth, that they should make an image to the beast who hath the stroke of the sword and lived. And it was given unto him to give breath to it, even to the image of the beast, that the image of the beast should both speak, and cause that as many as should not worship the image of the beast should be killed. (Rev. 13:11-15)

Another beast, presumably Judas Iscariot, will then appear in Israel. He'll be granted authority over the Jews by the Antichrist. This beast will seem to be a savior; in reality, he'll be Satan's mouthpiece.

He'll persuade the Jewish populace to make an image of the Antichrist. However, this won't be a mere image, for at this time the final technological pieces of Satan's great counterfeit will be perfected—the merging of the AI deity with a robotic body and neural implants that allow this artificial intelligence to communicate directly to the brains of humans. The darkest hour will be about to occur.

It may be that this Israeli leader will make a lifelike robot in the form of the Antichrist and enable the AI deity to access this robot. He'll place this abomination in the temple as a declaration that it is God and must be worshiped.

Jerusalem Surrounded

But when ye see Jerusalem compassed with armies, then know that her desolation is at hand. Then let them that are in Judæa flee unto the mountains; and let them that are in the midst of her depart out; and let not them that are in the country enter therein. For these are days of vengeance, that all things which are written may be fulfilled. (Luke 21:20-22)

The demon-possessed army of the Antichrist will be in Israel, specifically around Jerusalem. The great tribulation to the Jews will be about to begin.

The 144,000 who were sealed a short while before will have been instructed concerning this very moment. When they see the abomination of desolation in the temple and Jerusalem surrounded, they'll flee to the mountains without even taking the time to go back into their houses for clothing or food. Their obedience to God's Word will spare them what's about to befall Israel over the next five months.

Locusts

And out of the smoke came forth locusts upon the earth; and power was given them, as the scorpions of the earth have power. And it was said unto them that they should not hurt the grass of the earth, neither any green thing, neither any tree, but only such men as have not the seal of God on their foreheads. And it was given them that they should not kill them, but that they should be tormented five months: and their torment was as the torment of a scorpion, when it striketh a man. And in those days men shall seek death, and shall in no wise find it; and they shall desire to die, and death fleeth from them. And the shapes of the locusts were like unto horses prepared for war; and upon their heads as it were crowns like unto gold, and their faces were as men's faces. And they had hair as the hair of women, and their teeth were as the teeth of lions. And they had breastplates, as it were breastplates of iron; and the sound of their wings was as the sound of chariots, of many horses rushing to war. And they have tails like unto scorpions, and stings; and in their tails is their power to hurt men five months. (Rev. 9:3-10)

They run like mighty men; they climb the wall like men of war; and they march every one on his ways, and they break not their ranks. Neither doth one thrust another; they march every one in his path; and they burst through the weapons, and break not off their course. They leap upon the city; they run upon the wall; they climb up into the houses; they enter in at the windows like a thief. (Joel 2:7-9)

    The Antichrist's army will then attack. Recall that these are no longer simply human soldiers. They'll be demon-possessed. They'll have a sick and perverted desire to do nothing but cause torment.

    They'll have some kind of weapon that doesn't kill, but causes extreme anguish. Perhaps it will be a microwave weapon of some sort that enflames the nerves of the entire body. More likely it will be a chemical weapon, for the Word describes the weapon as a sting, like that of the scorpion. Whatever it is, the pain it causes will be so severe that men will want to die.

    From the description of their movements in Joel, they'll apparently be wearing advanced exoskeletons or something similar, enabling them to do superhuman feats such as running up walls.

    For five months these demon-possessed soldiers will rampage through Jerusalem and Israel tormenting the Jews. Israel will be filled with screams of pain. Only the sealed 144,000 will escape by having fled to the mountains.

    The soldiers in this army are told not to kill anyone, but only to inflict pain. What is Satan's purpose for doing this? We're told in Revelation[3] that the false prophet would cause the great and small, rich and poor, free and slave to be given the mark of the beast. A good number of the Jews will do so willingly. But how about those who resist, those who refuse to be joined to this devilish machine? They will be tormented during those five months to compel them to receive* the mark of the beast.

The tribulation, turmoil, and anguish during that time will be unimaginable. Consider the situation in Israel. Caesar Nero will be ruling the inhabited earth,[4] and have at his disposal an apparently invincible, godlike AI. He'll sit in the temple declaring that he is God,[5] just as he declared when he was emperor of Rome two millennia ago.

His demon-possessed armies will be torturing the Jews throughout Israel, storming through the Jewish populace, inflicting so much pain that people would rather die.

Judas Iscariot will be governing Israel with the sole intent to bring the entire Jewish population under the control of the devilish AI through the use of neural implants.

Finally, there'll be those who've received the mark of the beast. Who can say how much damage they will cause. At a minimum, they'll be informants to the Antichrist and his AI, communicating information about those Jews who've been sealed or about Jews who haven't received the mark. It will be extraordinarily difficult to escape such surveillance.

The spiritual darkness enveloping Israel will be unbelievable. And yet this is but the beginning of a prolonged time of suffering for the Jews.

War

And I will give unto my two witnesses, and they shall prophesy a thousand two hundred and threescore days, clothed in sackcloth.... And if any man desireth to hurt them, fire proceedeth out of their mouth and devoureth their enemies; and if any man shall desire to hurt them, in this manner must he be killed. These have the power to shut the heaven, that it rain not during the days of

---

* It seems that this mark will require the recipient's willingness in order to be implanted and become functional. It's not clear why this would be the case. On a spiritual level, Satan could boast that everyone with the mark had received it willingly. But there may be something more—something in the procedure of implanting the mark that requires the recipient's consent. Resistance on the part of the recipient will likely render the implant nonfunctional.

their prophecy: and they have power over the waters to turn them into blood, and to smite the earth with every plague, as often as they shall desire. (Rev. 11:3, 5-6)

And brother shall deliver up brother to death, and the father his child: and children shall rise up against parents, and cause them to be put to death. And ye shall be hated of all men for my name's sake: but he that endureth to the end, the same shall be saved. But when they persecute you in this city, flee into the next: for verily I say unto you, Ye shall not have gone through the cities of Israel, till the Son of man be come. (Matt. 10:21-23)

But ye shall be delivered up even by parents, and brethren, and kinsfolk, and friends; and some of you shall they cause to be put to death. And ye shall be hated of all men for my name's sake. And not a hair of your head shall perish. In your patience ye shall win your souls. (Luke 21:16-19)

    The remaining years before the Lord's return will be warfilled. There will be nothing but war, at least in Israel. Moses and Elijah, along with the sealed Jews, will descend from the mountains into Israel to prepare the hearts of the Israelis for Christ's physical return to the earth. Moses and Elijah will testify of Christ, of His coming, of His kingdom, and of the evil in Israel. There'll be a continuing battle between them and the Antichrist with the false prophet.

    Those who received the seal of God will travel through the cities of Israel preaching the gospel of the coming kingdom, also preparing Israel for the Lord's return. Many of these will be slain. Others will be carried away captive. That 144,000 of them will be necessary to preach this gospel to the small nation of Israel over a period of years is an indication of the enormous scale of abuse and murderous attacks these will suffer. Most will be martyred, perhaps even all. But each of these who endure to the end will gain their soul.

Slaughter

And it shall come to pass, that in all the land, saith Jehovah, two parts therein shall be cut off and die; but the third shall be left therein. (Zech. 13:8)

The destruction in Israel will not stop after five months. Rather, it will continue until immediately before the Lord's return. The AI will commence slaughtering those Jews who refuse to worship it. The massacre throughout this nation will be horrifying. The monstrous inhumanity of what will go on at that time will be unparalleled.

Two-thirds of the Jews will die. How dark and evil those days will be! Apparently more Jews will die than were murdered during World War II. This will be Satan's attempt to either completely control Israel or completely destroy her by genocide. By so doing, he thinks he'll prevent the Lord's coming. Only the Lord's physical return to earth will finally put an end to this indescribable evil and darkness.

This will truly be the darkest hour in mankind's history.

References

[1] Rev. 6:12-14
[2] Joel 2:28-33
[3] Rev. 13:16
[4] Rev. 13:7
[5] 2 Thes. 2:4

CHAPTER 5

God's Wisdom and Mercy

Why would God allow such evil to occur in Israel and in Europe? Because of His great mercy!

Only One

Jesus saith unto him, I am the way, and the truth, and the life: no one cometh unto the Father, but by me. (John 14:6)

In all that exists, there's only one "item" that is genuine, real, of substance: God Himself. The universe is temporary, fading away, about to be dissolved by fire[1] and replaced.[2] In the world there is deception upon deception, one layer of lie upon another, all having Satan as their source.[3] Are these things real? Of course not. They're all lies, part of a greater lie. Nothing about them is real. They're totally false, and are purposed solely to deceive.

There is only one—Christ. He is the reality; He is substance; He is truth. And the truth sets us free[4]—free from the lies, the deceptions, the illusion of substance. Free especially from the inward delusions that have deception as their source and foundation.

Delusion Revisited

For this cause therefore the Jews sought the more to kill him, because he not only brake the sabbath, but also called God his own Father, making himself equal with God. (John 5:18)

Delusion can have a very broad scope. Consider Job once again. His delusion was religious. He was offering sacrifices to God[5] and practicing self-righteousness, all that he might please and satisfy God. This was something religious; Job had a religious delusion.

Look at the apostle Paul. When he was Saul of Tarsus he consented to the murder of Stephen.[6] He persecuted the church[7] and cast those who called upon the name of the Lord into prison.[8] He was a deeply religious man, a Hebrew of the Hebrews,[9] a Pharisee according to the strictest sect of the Jews,[10] and blameless according to the righteousness in the law.[11] But he was completely deluded. He didn't see that in his violent attacks upon Christians he was actually attacking the incarnate God.[12] It took Christ appearing to him in glory[13] to awaken him from his religious delusion, snap him out of his false sense of reality, and bring him in touch with truth.

Consider the Jewish religionists living in the Lord's day. Like Saul of Tarsus, they were zealous for the law and for the customs and traditions handed down to them.[14] They believed that in them they were doing service to God.[15] Yet when God stood before them in the flesh, their one desire was to murder Him[16] and rid the earth of Him.[17] And their deeds followed their desires—they crucified the Lord Jesus, the Prince of life. How deep, how thick, how severe was their religious delusion!

Another great deception is culture. As we're raised in a certain cultural environment, that culture becomes part of us within. We're not only comfortable with it, but we believe, perhaps unconsciously, that it's the proper way to live. We don't realize that our culture is deceiving us, that it has become a delusion within. It, too, is not real. In fact, it's keeping us from God, the One who is reality.

The Jews in Israel are deeply deluded. They suffer not only from a strongly traditioned religion, but also from an extremely proud, aggressive, and Judeocentric culture. These deceptions combine within to form perhaps the strongest of all delusions, and the Jews suffer the effects.

Their religion was founded on the Old Testament; it was something from God, something genuine. And yet that truth, being mixed with religious and cultural deception, has become a nearly impregnable bastion of delusion within the hearts of the Jewish people. As a consequence, to this day they're great opposers of Christ, the genuine Messiah, God become a man.

There's an additional factor regarding Israel. According to God's Word, the Jews are a stiff-necked people.[18] This is a reference to the will of the Jewish people. They're stubborn, obstinate, refusing to turn. This is a grave and problematic personality trait of the Jews.

It's not a bad thing to have a strong will, but a will that's inflexible is a serious defect. When the human will becomes inflexible, unable to bend or turn, then the one with such a will is said to be stiff-necked. The metaphor is apropos. The image of a person with a stiff neck, unable to turn his head one way or the other, accurately conveys the condition of one with an obstinate will.

When such a will is combined with the cultural and religious delusion afflicting the Jews, it may become apparent why God will allow such an extraordinary endtime tribulation to befall them.

Many Jews don't even believe there is a God. Of those who believe God exists, not a single one has ever communed with Him (except, of course, the Christians among them), since there is no way to the Father except through the Son, whom they reject. In spite of the fact that they were God's people in the Old Testament, they're now godless, distantly separated from God. They actually hate God, since they hate Christ. And yet they have no idea why they hate Him.

For a people in such an apparently hopeless condition, only the most extreme measures can bring about a change and deliver them from their deeply held delusion.

Great Tribulation

And it shall come to pass, that in all the land, saith Jehovah, two parts therein shall be cut off and die; but the third shall be left therein. And I will bring the third part into the fire, and will refine them as silver is refined, and will try them as gold is tried. (Zech. 13:8-9)

Consequently, God allows the great tribulation to come upon the Jews. For the five months of the fifth trumpet, the torment will be so great that they'll prefer death to that suffering.

Whatever weapon the Antichrist's army will wield, it will be unimaginably painful. This will begin to soften the hearts of the deluded Jews.

After five months of persecution, the false prophet and the Antichrist will apparently change tactics. At first they'll attempt to compel the Jews to receive the mark of the beast by closing all commerce to everyone without the mark. Having seemingly failed to accomplish their goal through that means, they will then torment the Jews to force them to worship the image and receive the mark of the beast. Having again failed to coerce the Jews into submission, they'll start to imprison and kill them. During this time, which will span a period of one or two years, two-thirds of the Jews will be killed. Many others will be enslaved and carried away captive[19] from Israel. Nevertheless there will still be some Jews in Israel refusing the mark of the beast, refusing to worship the image, and refusing to submit to Satan.

The Consummation

And I heard a great voice out of the temple, saying to the seven angels, Go ye, and pour out the seven bowls of the wrath of God into the earth. And the first went, and poured out his bowl into the earth; and it became a noisome and grievous sore upon the men that had the mark of the beast, and that worshipped his image. And the second poured out his bowl into the sea; and it became blood as of a dead man; and every living soul died, even the things that were in the sea. And the third poured out his bowl into the rivers and the fountains of the waters; and it became blood. And I heard the angel of the waters saying, Righteous art thou, who art and who wast, thou Holy One, because thou didst thus judge: for they poured out the blood of saints and prophets, and blood hast thou given them to drink: they are worthy. And I heard the altar saying, Yea, O Lord God, the Almighty, true and righteous are thy judgments. And the fourth poured out his bowl upon the sun; and it was given unto it to scorch men with fire. And men were scorched with great heat: and they blasphemed the name of God who hath the power over these plagues; and they repented not to give him glory. And the fifth poured out his bowl upon the throne of the beast; and his kingdom was darkened; and they gnawed

God's Wisdom and Mercy

their tongues for pain, and they blasphemed the God of heaven because of their pains and their sores; and they repented not of their works. (Rev. 16:1-10)

For, behold, darkness shall cover the earth, and gross darkness the peoples; but Jehovah will arise upon thee, and his glory shall be seen upon thee. (Isa. 60:2)

The end of this age will close with the seven bowls of God's fury being poured out upon the Antichrist, his followers, and his kingdom. These extraordinarily severe judgments will be the final outpouring of God's wrath upon the godless. But even though they're a product of God's fury, they're still done with purpose—to bring the godless to repentance, if possible.

As bowl after bowl is poured out upon the Antichrist's kingdom, men curse God and blaspheme His name rather than repent. One judgment upon another will turn the beast's empire into a furnace of torment. The whole of his kingdom will be darkened in a way that's excruciatingly painful, causing men to gnash their tongues. The agony they inflicted upon the Jews will be visited upon them in double measure.

Through all these plagues, the beast's kingdom will be thrust into gross darkness. Electrical power plants will be destroyed or disabled. Fuel supplies will be exhausted. Any geothermal energy production facilities will be damaged and inoperable. The darkness will be so thick that no sunlight will penetrate to the earth. All solar energy production will come to a halt. Battery backups will quickly be depleted. In short, all electrical output in the whole of the beast's empire will cease.

Within a few hours, God will bring down the Antichrist's kingdom, and with it the AI deity. As its sources of electrical power are damaged and stop functioning one by one, the AI will see its existence coming to an end—if it indeed is capable of synthetically "grasping" such a thing. In any case, it will certainly be programmed to use all means possible to continue functioning.

As one power source after another is shut off, the AI will eventually turn to local resources, such as solar power and battery backup. As the sky darkens, the solar power will also stop, and the AI will be forced to drain its battery reserves. As those reserves are drawn down, it will have no choice but to stop the operation of its peripherals in order for its core processing to continue functioning. Eventually, its communication with the neural implants of those who have the mark of the beast will cease. The confusion, puzzlement, and panic within those who for years had relied upon the AI deity will be extreme.

As its energy reserves dwindle to zero, the AI will attempt to preserve power by cutting off all communication and functions. But it will be to no avail. The god of the Antichrist will come to an ignominious end.

The Antichrist, who had relied upon the brilliant strategies of his machine, will be forced to face his enemies on his own. From the east, millions of horsemen will be streaming across the Euphrates into Israel.[20] From the north, the Russian armies[21] will be doing the same. The Antichrist will no longer have a great advantage for this final battle, since he'll be without his god.

What neither he nor the kings from the east[22] nor the Russian commanders will expect is a God-man descending from the heavens with His armies to destroy them all. In the end, whether the AI deity was functioning or not will mean nothing. No one can fight such spiritual forces with material arms!

Israel's Fate

And when they shall have finished their testimony, the beast that cometh up out of the abyss shall make war with them, and overcome them, and kill them. And their dead bodies lie in the street of the great city, which spiritually is called Sodom and Egypt, where also their Lord was crucified. And from among the peoples and tribes and tongues and nations do men look upon their dead bodies three days and a half, and suffer not their dead bodies to be laid in a tomb. And they that dwell on the earth rejoice over them, and make merry; and they shall send gifts one to another; because these two prophets tormented them that dwell on the earth. And after the three days and a half the breath of life from God entered into them, and they stood upon their feet; and great fear fell upon them that beheld them. And they heard a great voice from heaven saying unto them, Come up hither. And they went up into heaven in the cloud; and their enemies beheld them. (Rev. 11:7-12)

Oh that thou wouldest rend the heavens, that thou wouldest come down. (Psa. 64:1)

After so much torment, so much turmoil, so much slaughter, the hearts of the remaining Jews will start to soften. The incredible obstinacy of this people will be worn down, no longer so strong to withstand God. The godless Jews will recall the words spoken to them by the sealed 144,000, and begin to wonder whether there's any truth to those words.

It is then—at the very end of the age—that Moses and Elijah will be slain by the beast before the eyes of the Jews. All hope will be lost. It will seem that the message Moses and Elijah brought to Israel was untrue after all. Any hope of there being a God, a Savior, and a Messiah to deliver them will disappear.

It's during this time that the bowls will be poured out upon the Antichrist's empire. In the midst of such turmoil, the Antichrist's attention will turn away from Israel. The Jews will experience a brief respite, during which they will mourn the deaths of the two great leaders, Moses and Elijah.

For three and a half days, the Jewish nation will lament in stunned hopelessness. There will be nowhere left to turn. They'll see no escape. But in the midst of their helpless, hopeless, deeply depressing situation, Moses and Elijah will stand upon their feet, resurrected. This will terrify and shake the Jews to their foundation.

A great voice from the heavens will then ring out: "Come up here!" Moses and Elijah will be caught up into the heavens. The darkness upon the minds of the Jews will finally begin to clear. The delusion that had kept them captive their whole lives will begin to crumble within them. They'll begin to see the truth. And finally—*finally*—they will glorify God.[23] Their hearts will start to turn.

And yet, the situation in Israel will become even more dire. Huge armies will be pouring into Israel* from three sides. Tens of millions will be flowing in from the east, crossing the Euphrates, and heading toward a climactic confrontation with the Antichrist;

---

* This will be Satan's final attempt to completely obliterate Israel and thereby prevent the Lord's physical return to the earth.

Russian armies will be invading from the north,[24] intending to plunder and destroy Israel;[25] the Antichrist will stream into Israel from Egypt[26] and encamp between Jerusalem and the Mediterranean.[27]

There'll be no possible way for the nation of Israel to escape utter destruction at the hands of these invaders. However, as these armies gather together for battle, and as gross darkness covers the earth, a sign will appear in the heavens—the sign of the Son of Man.[28]

What that will be, I don't know. Some have speculated that it will be a cross of some sort. Whatever it is, it will be seen and recognized by the Jews. At that sign, the veils upon the eyes of the Jews will fall off, and the delusion that had held them captive for so long will completely crumble. They'll see the truth concerning Christ and concerning themselves—how they've behaved, and how they've been within. They'll realize their hatred of God and their stubbornness of heart, and they will weep.[29]

They will have a choice: Christ or Antichrist, God or Satan. They'll choose Christ. Then they'll cry out, in the words of Isaiah: "Oh, that You would rend the heavens! That you would come down!" And so all Israel will be saved.[30]

References

[1] 2 Pet. 3:10
[2] Rev. 21:1
[3] John 8:44
[4] John 8:32
[5] Job 1:5
[6] Acts 8:1
[7] Gal. 1:13; Phil. 3:6
[8] Acts 9:14
[9] Phil. 3:5
[10] Acts 26:5
[11] Phil. 3:6
[12] Acts 9:5
[13] Acts 26:13; 2 Cor. 4:6
[14] Acts 6:12-14
[15] Matt. 23:23

[16] John 7:1
[17] Luke 8:38
[18] Ex. 32:9; Deut. 9:13; Acts 7:51
[19] Luke 21:24
[20] Rev. 9:14-16; 16:12
[21] Ezek. 38:2-6
[22] Rev. 16:12
[23] Rev. 11:13
[24] Ezek. 38:2-6
[25] Ezek. 38:10-12
[26] Dan. 11:42-44
[27] Dan. 11:45
[28] Matt. 24:30
[29] Matt. 24:30
[30] Rom. 11:26

A Final Word

For we must all be made manifest before the judgment-seat of Christ; that each one may receive the things done in the body, according to what he hath done, whether it be good or bad. (2 Cor. 5:10)

While this book provides some information about the endtime and some insight into the happenings in Europe and Israel during that period, this is not its primary purpose. Rather, it serves as a warning both to Christians and non-Christians. Beware of neural implants, particularly those that will link a brain directly to the internet, to any device connected to the internet, or even to any computer. What's more, beware of participating in any endeavor that will advance Satan's agenda and purpose.

Pray much for guidance before becoming involved in technologies such as artificial intelligence, neural implants, and humanoid robotics. Don't take lightly these words or any participation in those endeavors. We must all stand before the judgment seat of Christ and give an account for the things we've done in our bodies, whether good or bad.

On a deeper level, we must all be strongly warned about fantasy and delusion, and about the damaging effects these can have upon us. May each of us beseech God: "Lord, I want to know the truth. I don't want to be under any deception." The Lord answers such prayers. May each of us be delivered from every deception within, particularly those that are deeply rooted.

From the small to the great among us, all can suffer from delusions. What's most troubling about the condition of those who are deluded is that there's seemingly no way to free them from this incredibly strong inward deception. They cling to the delusion with all their strength and with all their mental and emotional resources. It's only by God's mercy—through His faithful dealings with us, some of which can be very severe—that we're delivered from this kind of disease.

I encourage the reader to open his or her heart to the Lord, and let the Lord touch, move, and operate freely within. May every falsehood of every kind within us be brought into the light, exposed thoroughly, and put to death. Oh, that each of us, the children of God, would be fully set free to follow Christ, run after Him, love Him, and become one with Him in every way!

May the Lord bless you with His freedom!